The Johnstown Flood of 1889: The Story of the Deadliest Flood in American History

By Charles River Editors

Flood debris near the Pennsylvania Railroad bridge

About Charles River Editors

Charles River Editors provides superior editing and original writing services across the digital publishing industry, with the expertise to create digital content for publishers across a vast range of subject matter. In addition to providing original digital content for third party publishers, we also republish civilization's greatest literary works, bringing them to new generations of readers via ebooks.

Introduction

A 19th century engraving depicting flood damage

The Johnstown Flood of 1889

"The deluge released by the dam's collapse carried more than 12,000 cubic meters of debris-filled water each second. Flow rates in the Mississippi River typically vary between 7,000 and 20,000 cubic meters per second." – Sid Perkins, *Science News*, Vol.176

In 2005, the world watched in horror as Hurricane Katrina decimated New Orleans, and the calamity seemed all the worse because many felt that technology had advanced far enough to prevent such tragedies, whether through advanced warning or engineering. However, the failure of human engineering like that seen in New Orleans was nothing new, and it had previously had even deadlier consequences in Johnstown, Pennsylvania.

Although floods rarely get as much coverage as other kinds of natural disasters like volcanic explosions, the Johnstown Flood of 1889 has remained an exception due to the sheer destruction and magnitude of the disaster. On May 31, 1889, Johnstown became a casualty of a combination of heavy rains and the failure of the South Fork Dam to stem the rising water levels of Lake Conemaugh about 15 miles away. The dam's inability to contain the water and its subsequent collapse resulted in a catastrophic flood that swept through the town with virtually no warning. With water flowing at a rate equivalent to the Mississippi River, a tide of water and debris 60 feet high and traveling 40 miles per hour in some places surged through Johnstown and swept away people and property alike. The flood ultimately resulted in the deaths of over 2,000 people and destroyed thousands of buildings, wreaking damages estimated to be the equivalent of nearly half a billion dollars today.

In 1889, the Johnstown Flood was the deadliest natural disaster in American history, and though it was later surpassed by other events, the unprecedented nature of the flood led to relief efforts never before seen, including by the Red Cross. The Johnstown Flood also led to a change in laws as people tried and failed to recoup damages caused by the collapse of the dam and the subsequent flood.

The Johnstown Flood of 1889 chronicles the story America's deadliest natural disaster during the 19th century. Along with pictures of important people, places, and events, you will learn about the Johnstown Flood like never before, in no time at all.

The Johnstown Flood of 1889: The Story of the Deadliest Flood in American History

About Charles River Editors

Introduction

Chapter 1: A Balmy Day in May

"On a balmy day in May,
When bright nature held full sway
And the birds sang sweetly in the sky above
A lovely city lay serene,
In a valley deep in green,
Where thousands dwelt in happiness and love" - Joseph Flynn, "The Johnstown Flood"

On the morning of May 29, 1889, Johnstown, Pennsylvania was the quintessential American small town. Settled by Swiss German immigrants during the last days of America's colonial period, it was officially chartered in 1800 and named for the Johns family. Once the Pennsylvania Main Line Canal was dug in the early 1830s, the town became an important transfer point for items being shipped to and from the area, and it also was an important railroad hub, first for the Allegheny Portage Railroad and later for the Pennsylvania Railroad. English author Charles Dickens even mentioned it while touring America in 1842.

By the time the Civil War broke out in 1861, Johnstown was the place where the Pennsylvania connected with the Baltimore & Ohio Railroad. This led to widespread prosperity for the city, especially after the Cambria Iron Company opened in 1860. For the next several decades, Johnstown was a major steel producer, outpacing even nearby Pittsburgh.

On that May morning in 1889, Johnstown's main claim to fame was that she was the barbed wire capital of the United States. While this might not sound like a big deal, it is important to remember that this distinction existed during the heyday of the American West, when cattle herders and farmers alike depended on the inexpensive and quick construction of fencing material. The local Cambria Works owned 40,000 acres of rich countryside, from which it mined coal, iron, and limestone. She was the city's biggest business, employing 7,000 of the city's more than 20,000 citizens.

14 miles north of Johnstown lay the small community of South Fork. During the 1840s, while she was busy building canals to improve travel across the state, the Commonwealth of Pennsylvania dammed up the Conemaugh River, building the South Fork Dam and creating Lake Conemaugh. Originally intended to be a water reservoir for the Main Line of Public Works, it was sold by the state to the Pennsylvania Railroad in 1853. It changed hands several more times over the following decades, until the South Fork Fishing and Hunting Club bought it in 1879. The club's members, including Andrew Carnegie and Robert Pitcairn, developed the area as a rural retreat for themselves and their families. While the club's wealthy founders poured thousands of dollars into making the buildings on the club compound comfortable, they spent very little on maintaining the dam. As a result, the structure was subject to decay and frequent leaks.

In 1880, Daniel Morrell, the owner of the Cambria Iron Works and a member of the club, became concerned about the dam's condition and sent engineer John Fulton to inspect it. Fulton then issued a report that included the following concerns:

> "It is evident, therefore, that the water cannot overturn, or slide, the dam out, enmasse—

> There appear to me two serious elements of danger in the dam:

> 1st. The want of a discharge pipe to reduce or take the water out of the dam for needed repairs.

> 2nd. The unsubstantial method of repair, leaving a large leak, which appears to be cutting the new embankment.

> As the water cannot be lowered, the difficulty arises of reaching the source of the present destructive leaks. At present there is 40 feet of water in the dam, when the full head of 60 feet is reached, it appears to me to be only a question of time until the former cutting is repeated. Should this break be made during a season of flood, it is evident that considerable damage would ensue along the line of the Conemaugh.

> It is impossible to estimate how disastrous this flood would be, as its force would depend on the size of the breach in the dam with proportional rapidity of discharge.

> The stability of the dam can only be assured by a thorough overhauling of the present lining on the upper slope, and the construction of an ample discharge pipe to reduce or remove the water to make necessary repairs."

Tragically, these repairs were never made. Instead, when Morrell presented the report to his fellow club members, they dismissed it, citing the following, largely trivial errors as reasons to not pay any attention to it.

> "Error 1. Organization is not the Sportsmen's Association of Western Pennsylvania.

> Error 2. Dam not originally built of stone, face of dam on lake was not rip-rapped.

> Error 3. Large arched culvert did not contain pipes but three large conduits which terminated in the wooden tower in the lake, rods and valves then regulated the flow of water from the dam.

> Error 4. Fulton claimed the dam was destroyed when the bulkheads burned. Impossible while the dam held. Would burn only to the water's edge. Dam destroyed by the arch culvert giving way in center of embankment.

Error 5. Fulton claimed that the break created a notch 200 feet long and 40 feet deep, - break went clean to the bottom."

Still concerned, Morrell next requested that the Pennsylvania Railroad send someone out to look the dam over. Concerned, the railroad sent two men, who in turn issued conflicting reports about the dam's security. Wanting to err on the side of caution, Morrell wrote a letter to the club's president, Benjamin Ruff, urging him to reconsider. The letter read, in part, "We do not wish to put any obstruction in the way of your accomplishing your object in the reconstruction of the dam; but we must protest against the erection of a dam at that place, that will be a perpetual menace to the lives and property of those residing in the upper valley of the Conemaugh from its insecure construction. In my judgment there should have been provided some means by which the water could be let out of the dam in case of trouble, and I think that you will find it necessary to provide an outlet pipe or gate before any engineer could pronounce the job a safe one. If this dam could be securely reconstructed with a safe means of driving off the water in case any weakness manifests itself, I should regard the accomplishment of this work a very desirable one, and if some arrangement could be made with your Association by which the store of water in this reservoir could be used in time of great drought in the mountains, this Company would be willing to cooperate with you in the work, and contribute liberally toward making the dam absolutely safe."

In spite of his best efforts, Morrell was unable to make any headway with the club's leadership before he passed away in 1885.

As a result of the dam's poor condition, warnings of an imminent dam break were part of daily life in Johnstown. During the early 1880s, alarms were regularly sounded and, at first, the town's citizens reacted quickly, taking to the hills and higher ground around the town. However, as time went on and one false alarm followed another, the population became jaded. By 1889, the only people who reacted were those new to the city.

Chapter 2: The Scene Was Changed

"Ah, but soon the scene was changed,
For just like a thing deranged,
A storm came crashing through the quiet town
The wind, it raved and shrieked,
Thunder rolled and lightning streaked,
And the rain it poured in awful torrents down." – Joseph Flynn, "The Johnstown Flood"

It all started with a storm, not in Pennsylvania, but in the Midwest, where dark clouds gathered over Kansas and Nebraska toward the end of May 1889. Farmers watched the sky with concern, as it was near the harvest time for wheat. A little rain would do no harm, but a bad storm, especially one accompanied by hail, could be disastrous. This time the wheat was safe; this storm would take lives, not bread. Instead of remaining over the American prairies, it blew east, toward the hill country of northern Pennsylvania, arriving there on May 30. And there it remained, hour after dreadful hour.

At first, no one paid much attention to the rain. The farmers may have been thankful for it, for the crops were just beginning to sprout out of the ground and extra rain was welcome. They became concerned as time passed. It would not be good if the plants washed away. The city's fathers and the town's children also watched the rain, hoping it would end before the annual Memorial Day parade. The few veterans of the Civil War who always marched in that event had been polishing their medals and trimming their beards. It was a big event that everyone looked forward to.

Fortunately, the rain did stop briefly on the morning of the 30th, and the parade went on as planned. Of course, there were some whispered concerns, as many of the lower parts of town were flooded and had several or more feet of water standing in their streets But flooding was nothing new in the community and those who were truly anxious went ahead and moved their most valuable possessions to the upper rooms in their homes. They assumed that if the water did indeed rise again, it would simply flow through the empty floors as it had in the past. The women were dreading cleaning up the mess it would leave behind, but after all, they reasoned, such was a woman's lot in life.

Meanwhile, up at the South Fork Dam, Elias Unger was concerned. The river outside his window was more swollen than he had ever seen it. Slipping on a raincoat, he dashed outside into the rain to get a better look. Walking along the road that ran the length of the dam, he saw that the water was nearly to the top. Hoping to unclog the spillway that was trapping the water on the other side of the dam's wall, he called together a group of men. Together they worked through the morning, pulling out everything from broken fish traps to tree limbs. At the same time, others worked with shovels, frantically attempting to create another spillway on the other side of the dam, in the hopes of relieving some of the pressure on the leaking structure. When these efforts failed, they all turned their attention to piling earth and rock on the road itself, in the hopes of raising the wall and preventing the water from flowing over it.

David Brossard's picture of Unger's house today

What few, if any, realized that day was that this was not an ordinary rainfall, nor was it over. The last blast of the city band had hardly faded when the rain started again. It rained all night. The water crept higher and higher into homes; creeks became lakes, and streams became rivers. By daybreak, the nearby Conemaugh River was out of its banks, and water was indeed creeping through homes in Johnstown. As the sun rose, some members of the population were becoming concerned that this was more than just a heavy rainfall. C.C. Ramsey later wrote, "I arose at the usual hour, and found the waters rising very rapidly – so fast, in fact, that the water covered the first floor before we had time to remove carpets and furniture to the upper floors, at the same time forcing the entire family to the second floor. At the hour of 10 A.M. we were surrounded by at least ten feet of water, which closed all channels of escape from that hour, as the current which swept through the street was so strong that any ordinary boat could make no progress against it. However, a boat was a luxury that we did not possess. After 11 A.M. all was quiet even to the stillness of death; one could hear the swash of the waters, the voices of neighbors, or the bark of a dog."

People's suspicions were confirmed as word spread across town that the telegraph lines were down. Much of the local railroad track was underwater, and many were concerned that the afternoon train would not be able to get into town. As the day wore on, some people said that the track had washed away entirely, while others complained about uprooted trees falling over, endangering life and property. The housewives were now concerned about more than water getting into their homes; they also were having to deal with the trash from the previous day's parade being washed into downstairs parlors.

Then there were the animals. While house pets could join their owners upstairs, farm animals had to be protected. Victor Heiser later wrote, "During the afternoon of the thirty-first the overflow from the river crept steadily higher, inch by inch, through the streets of the town. Although it had not yet reached the stable, which stood on higher ground than the house, my father became concerned over the safety of his fine pair of horses which were tied in their stalls, and suggested that I make a dash for the stable and unfasten them. The rain was falling so hard that I was almost drenched as I plowed my laborious way through the two feet of water."

Word of the flooding began to spread outside the city, as those who had business in town attempted to make their way to local merchants, only to be turned away by the water. A Mrs. S.W. Fields told of her experience in learning about the mess: "In the morning Charlie came home from town; told me he could not get to Johnstown office for high water, and then it was eight feet at Sandy Vale Cemetery. I was not surprised at all, knowing that was a most frequent occurrence. So we waited and watched the water until in the afternoon (Charlie staying at home). Then I proposed that the children and myself go up to Canan's to see what the water looked like. It was then coming into my yard. It was all the dry ground on that side of the street. The thought struck me that I had better make ourselves comfortable, for we might not get back; yet at the same time I never dreamed that we would be washed out. But I paid attention to the monitor and made us all comfortable, and the clothes we put on we wore for weeks after."

Chapter 3: Like the Paul Revere of Old

"Like the Paul Revere of old,
Comes a rider brave and bold,
On a big bay horse he's flying like a deer
And he is shouting warnings shrill,
'Quickly fly off to the hills,'
But the people smile and show no signs of fear" – Joseph Flynn, "The Johnstown Flood"

As the rain continued, those who had lived in the city for a while began to talk about the dam. Some knew that it had been repaired many times and may have even whispered concerns about its safety. However, most of the citizens had no idea just how much danger they were in. After all, the dam had stood solidly by for decades; there was no need to be overly concerned about it.

Unger had called in John Parke, a local engineer, to see if he had any suggestions as to what might be done. At first, Parke thought that it might help if they focused their efforts on cutting a hole through one edge of the dam, but he soon discounted this idea. Still, everyone kept working, with each hoping that he might somehow be the one who would come up with an idea to save the dam. By 1:30 that afternoon, however, it was clear that there was nothing else they could do. Unger ordered everyone off the dam and to the higher ground nearby. There, they would wait for a miracle that never came.

Concerned about what was going on at the dam, the Reverend G.W. Brown, pastor of the United Brethren Church in South Fork, walked over to the area from his home and joined those waiting. After the disaster, he wrote the following in a letter to a friend: "The lake was a little over two miles south of our village, and, by the water course, fifteen miles from Johnstown. It covered 750 acres of ground, and had an average depth of over 30 feet. Having heard the rumor that the reservoir was leaking, I went up to see for myself. It then wanted ten minutes of 3 o'clock in the afternoon of Friday, May 31st. When I approached, the water was running over the breast of the dam to the depth of about a foot. The first break in the earthen surface made a few minutes later was large enough to admit the passage train of cars. When I witnessed that, I exclaimed, 'God have mercy on the people below,' but I did not then suppose that the destruction of the lake would be attended by so great a loss of human life. The dam melted away, oh, how quickly! Only a few moments were required to make an opening more than 300 feet wide and down to the bottom. I watched it until the wall that held back the waters was torn away, and the entire lake began to move, and until, finally, with a tremendous rush that made the hills quake, the vast body of water was poured out into the valley below. Only about 45 minutes were required to precipitate those millions of tons of water upon the unsuspecting inhabitants of the Conemaugh Valley; and right here it began its work of destruction."

While he and his men were working, Unger had ordered warnings to be sent via telegraph to all the cities below the dam. However, these warnings were largely ignored. As the day wore on, the flooding brought down the telegraph wires, making further communication impossible. By the time Reverend Brown made his observations at 2:50 PM, there was little time for anyone to escape. The flood hit South Fork first, but because the town was on higher ground than Johnstown, it had not experienced the same level of flooding. Still, as Brown related, it was a horrific sight: "A mill, house and stable, owned by George Fisher, were demolished in an instant. Fortunate it was for him that, a few minutes before, he and his family had moved to higher ground. He had conveyed a milk wagon, a plow and other implements to a more elevated spot, supposing they would be safe there; but the mighty rush of water leaped over the hills and carried off his and other people's property, to be seen no more. It was but an instant apparently before the mighty torrent tossed into the air the iron bridge that spanned the South Fork, and crushed, beyond recognition, the house and two barns belonging to George Lamb. Onward dashed the destructive flood, roaring like a mighty battle, tree-top high, toward South Fork village, rolling over and over again rocks that weighed tons and tons, carrying them a mile or more from the spot where they had lain for ages."

Most of the houses in the area were destroyed, but because the flood had not yet picked up any debris, only four people were killed. The others were able to escape in time to higher ground.

Emma Ehrenfeld, the telegraph operator for South Fork, later wrote, "About 3 o'clock or probably a minute or two after, as I was sitting there, of course we were waiting for [the train], and the engineer and the conductor of the 1165 were in the office at the time, and it seems were looking out of the window; I was sitting with my back to the window; and they said, "Look at the people running! I wonder what's wrong." I looked up and went to the window, and just then, it seemed the cry arose that it was coming, and he looked out of the window and said something about the reservoir going, and he and the conductor started down stairs. I then went to the window and looked out and saw people running, and some were screaming, and some hollowed for me to come, and I looked out of the window on the side of the river, and saw it coming. Of course, I can't describe it to you...."

Tragically, a train was nearing the area when the dam gave way. John Hess, the engineer on the train, heard the water and saw what was happening. Heroically, he tied down his train's whistle and pushed his engineers to the breaking point to speed backwards through East Conemaugh, then Franklin and Woodvale and finally, Conemaugh, warning as many people as he could of the coming disaster: "It was like a hurricane through a wooded country. It was a roar and a crash and a smash; I can't tell what it was like, but the first thing I heard was a terrible roar in the hollow and the next thing was a crash something like a big building going to pieces, which I think was the company house that stood right up around the curve, and the trees and brush hid it from our sight. I couldn't see it, but there was people told me afterwards that that house crushed together just about the time we left. We saw no flood; we saw a drift of large logs in the river, but the river was no higher than it was 20 minutes before that. I pulled the whistle wide open, and went into Conemaugh that way."

By this time, a number of large businesses in the area were also sounding the alarm, letting others know something bad was happening. With the rain falling in torrents, it took very little time to guess the worst. J.C. Walkinshaw, the yard master at East Conemaugh later wrote, "I had just sat down about a minute, I heard a whistle blow... She gave four or five long blasts. That meant to me that there was danger. I jumped off of my chair, and as soon as I heard the second blast, I ran out and hollowed for every person to go away off the road and get on high ground, and I started up the track. Just as I left the office, I saw the rear end of this work train backing around the curve. I started up toward the train, and the minute I saw the train stop, I saw the engineer jump off and run for the hill. Just at that minute, I saw a large wave come around the hill. When I saw it, it was a body of water in a swell, apparently to me about four feet higher than the track where I was standing. As soon as I saw it come every person was making for the hill, and the distance I had to go, I started to save myself..."

A picture of the dam after its collapse

Chapter 4: E're They Turned Away

"Ah, but e're they turned away,
The brave rider and his bay,
And the many thousand souls he tried to save
For they had no time to spare,
Or to offer up a pray'r,
They were hurled at once into a wat'ry grave." – Joseph Flynn, "The Johnstown Flood"

The first major item that stood in the way of the growing wall of water and debris was the Conemaugh Viaduct, a railroad bridge that stood almost 80 feet above the river below. For a short time, the floating mountain was stopped and tangled against the viaduct's elegant arch. However, the debris soon formed a new dam, trapping the water on the other side. While this offered many people a few more precious minutes of life, it also created a pressure that quickly built like champagne in a shaken bottle. After just seven minutes of increasing pressure, the viaduct collapsed. The flood shot out beneath it with more force than it had had before, slamming into the next small community on its murderous path, Mineral Point. Within minutes, only one large boulder was left in a town that had once housed 30 families.

Rushing past Mineral Point, the flood next hit East Conemaugh. D.M. Montgomery, the telegraph operator there, later said, "…it was just a mountain of water coming down, full of trees, houses, and everything; and the water seemed to be rolling over and over, and just crushing everything in front of it. If it struck anything, you never saw it after that."

After passing through East Conemaugh, the flood flowed on through Woodvale, where it took away George Barbour's home and family. He later wrote this heartrending account to what family he had left: "My mother, my wife, and three children were all drowned. I have been almost crazy. I even did not think of writing to any of my friends. For a week I was kept busy trying to find their bodies. I had to climb the hills to get from one morgue to the other, and had no one to help me. Most of the time I had only one meal a day, and became so weak and sick that I had to stop. I found my dear wife and dear little girl. I had to carry the coffins over a mile to where the bodies were. As the bridges were all washed away I had to get a wagon and drive four miles over the hills to the cemetery, and it was 8 o'clock in the evening when I got there. It was the hardest thing ever any man did, to put his own dear wife and child in a coffin and bury them himself; but it was the only thing I could do, and hundreds of others had to do the same."

As is so often the case, grief came to Barbour with its best friend, guilt, as he wrestled, as so many would for the rest of their lives, with what he might have done differently. He continued, "I could not find my poor dear mother and two little boys. One was about 7 years old and the other was our baby, about 3 months old. It was so nice, and everybody said it was the brightest and prettiest baby they had ever seen. Oh, if I had only stayed at home with them! I had taken them up to my sister-in-law's and told them to stay until I came back. I went to town and stayed longer than I intended to. It got clear and stopped raining, and they went back down town to our home, but could not get out any more. I was on my way home when the dam broke. I tried to reach the bridge, but when I was about a hundred yards from it, it gave way. I ran up the hill and saw my house and all the rest of the houses in our part of town move off. The roofs were filled with men, women and children, but they could do nothing. It didn't leave a house in Woodvale."

While moving through Woodvale, the flood also washed through the Cambria Iron Works, picking up bundles of recently made barbed wire, adding that deadly ingredient to the collecting debris. Nearly a third of the city's 1,100 residents were killed. The boilers at the Gautier Wire Works blew up, sending clouds of black smoke into the air. Colonel John P. Linton reported, "Shortly before 4 o'clock we heard the loud and doleful whistling of the engines at the mill, which surely betokens a fire, and which we at the time supposed to be such an alarm. I have been informed since that this was intended to warn people that the South Fork dam had burst, and to prepare for the consequences. To us, even if we had understood the purpose of the alarm, it could have been of no avail, as an impassable flood of water already isolated our house, and we could not have fled to any place of refuge."

Finally, nearly an hour after the dam gave way, the flood finally reached Johnstown. Charles R. Phipps was fortunate that he was home when the alarm sounded. He later wrote, "This was about 4 P.M. In a few minutes the water began to enter the room. We started to take up the carpets, but in less than half a minute someone burst into the room, exclaiming "The reservoir has broken; get up stairs, quick! Quick!" We did not get there too soon, for as we rushed up the stairs the house opposite crushed into ours, and behind it was a great wall of water bearing on its surface, houses, trees, cars and almost every other imaginable object. From the second floor we saw a three-story brick house fall to the ground. Our house moved off with the current, and, as it went, two walls of the room we were in fell. I jumped for the window of the house next door to ours, and from there to the roof; but as it started off and seemed about to roll over, I sprang into the waters to reach what was left of ours. As I got on it the roof fell in, and we crawled to a pile of drift that was whirling by. It lodged some hundred feet from the front street and we got to the floor of a brick house which was poised at an angle of about forty-five degrees. I helped the others up (three ladies and two gentlemen)."

Chapter 5: The Cry of Distress

"Then the cry of distress,
Rings from East to the West,
And our whole dear country now is plunged in woe
For the thousands burned and drowned
In the city of Johnstown,
All were lost in the great overflow." – Joseph Flynn, "The Johnstown Flood"

Picture of a damaged house in Johnstown

By the time the tidal wave released by the dam arrived in Johnstown, the water and debris were moving at nearly 40 miles per hour, and there was just too little time to escape. In all, about 20,000,000 tons of water rushed through the valley over the next hour, destroying everything in its path. Had it just destroyed the forests and buildings that it encountered, there would not have been so much damage. However, the flood was like a naughty child, running away with everyone's toys and carrying more and more material with it as it moved. Victor Heiser recalled, "I had loosed the horses and was about to leave the shelter of the doorway when my ears were stunned by the most terrifying noise I had ever heard in my sixteen years of life. The dreadful roar was punctuated with a succession of tremendous crashes. I stood for a moment, bewildered and hesitant. I could see my mother and my father standing at an upper window in the house. My father, frantic with anxiety over my safety, was motioning me urgently toward the top of the building. Fortunately, I had made a passageway only a few days before to the red tin roof, so that some necessary repairs could be made. Thus it was only a matter of seconds before I was up on the ridge. From my perch I could see a huge wall advancing with incredible rapidity down the diagonal street. It was not recognizable as water, it was a dark mass in which seethed houses, freight cars, trees, and animals. As this wall struck Washington Street broadside, my boyhood home was crushed like an eggshell before my eyes, and I saw it disappear. I wanted to know how long it would take me to get to the other world, and in the split second before the stable was hit, I looked at my watch. It was exactly four-twenty. But, instead of being shattered, the big barn was ripped from its foundations and began to roll, like a barrel, over and over. Stumbling, crawling, and racing, I somehow managed to keep on top."

Anyone not inside a sturdy building was killed instantly by the water and the debris. Even those who were excellent swimmers stood no chance, as they were more likely to be pummeled to death by the lumber and limbs swirling around them than to drown. C.C. Ramsey wrote, "The roar of the mighty wave fell upon our ears, and with one impulse we rushed to the third floor, which we gained just in time, as at that instant a string of flat cars, coupled together, struck the house, demolishing the two lower floors, leaving us the mansard, which floated toward the stone bridge. During this time we, with great difficulty, reached the roof, upon which we remained until we wedged into the debris ... within a few hundred yards of the Morrell Institute. It is beyond description; we can hardly remember, only we climbed over many houses, floating roofs, piles of debris, and finally the haven of safety was reached. During this time there continued a cold, driving rain which chilled one to the marrow."

The Stone Bridge that Ramsey referred to was the only structure to be hit by the wave of debris and survive. Even that quickly proved to be both a blessing and a curse. Many were able to escape by crawling across the debris that soon became trapped against the bridge. However, the water soon built up to such a level that it flowed over the bridge to flood a different part of town. W.M. Hayes, the division supervisor for the Pennsylvania Railroad whose tracks the bridge supported, later testified, "In the meantime, Johnstown Lumber Company's boom had broken up on Stony Creek, up above Johnstown, and the drift was coming down very rapidly, and we with our force were trying to keep the bridge clear; -- that is, the stone bridge west of Johnstown, and we worked away there until about 4:10. The water had receded, we believe, about two inches. About 4:10, our attention was attracted by people shouting, and I saw this bank of water and drift coming down the Conemaugh, almost like a wall. About 4:10, it crossed the town before it reached our bridge, and went up into what is called Kernville, a suburb of Johnstown, on Stony

Creek, then after it got level there, it came down to our bridge. It was a very short time, but we saw the course of it."

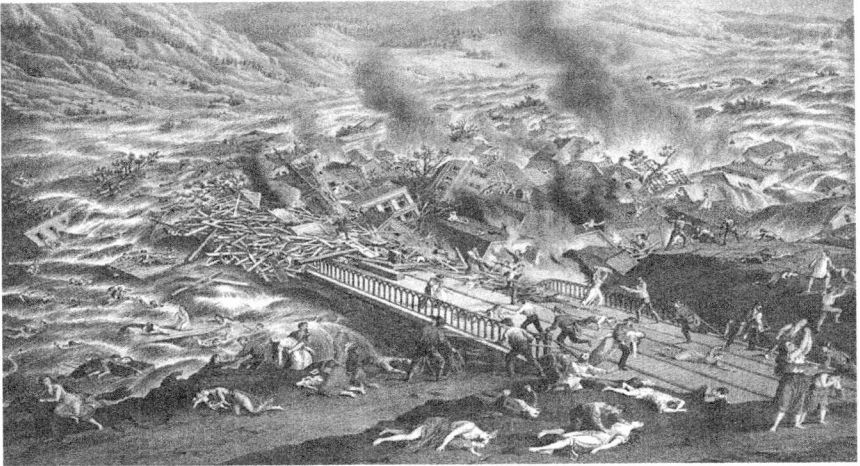

A 19ᵗʰ century illustration depicting the flood and the Stone Bridge

Picture of the Stone Bridge and nearby debris after the flood

Because of the way in which the bridge rerouted the water, there were a few people living near it who had the dubious honor of witnessing all the destruction the disaster wrought without actually being in danger themselves. One of these fortunate few was Louise Mueller, a single woman living near enough to the bridge to see a sight she would never forget: "Thrusting my head through an open window, and looking north-easterly, from which direction seemed to be coming an awful something, I saw what filled me with indescribable horror. A mountain of darkness from the very heavens down was pushing over on us, bringing houses and trees – a great mass of everything. The atmosphere was filled with spray, clouds of dust, flying particles of all kinds. My first impression was that the heavy clouds had broken down at the end of the heavens, and that the whole mass was gradually lowering. Then I wondered it if could be a cyclone, or of the nature of one, since there was such a strong breeze. We never for a moment thought of Lake Conemaugh; and, if we had, I presume we would not have decided that was it; for this dark, cloudlike mass, bearing down upon us with everything before it, had not yet dissolved itself into anything, so far as we could see. The fast rising of the waters I attributed to the fact that they were accumulating because of the pressure of this immense body of something."

The flood not only produced a sense of danger, but it also created an unbelievable scene of destruction, as if an angry child was kicking down a city he had just built of blocks. Mueller continued, "For several seconds we stood looking upon the moving mass before us. A good part of our city, in wreck and ruin, was sweeping out Market Street toward the Stoney Creek, almost immediately in front of us. Directly everything about us began to bend and sway like so many twigs. The crashing and creaking of the falling homes; the crunching of the moving particles driven by this black cloud; the dark waters about our feet; our own sensations as if all things, even old earth herself, moving off, getting away from us. By this time the dark mass of cloud had disappeared. A great body of water was rushing madly about, tearing westward on the north side of us, and rushing eastward on the south side, apparently a perfect whirlpool, and carrying wreckage with it to which the people were clinging. It was perfectly awful to see the people sweeping by on portions of their homes and fragments of all kinds, and with scarcely a hope of escape, entirely unable to steer their crafts to safety."

Picture of damage

Chapter 6: A Scene No Tongue Can Tell

"T'was a scene no tongue can tell,
Homes strewn about pell-mell,
Infants torn away from loving mother's arms
And strong men battling for their lives,
Husbands struggling for their wives,
And no one left protecting them from harm" – Joseph Flynn, "The Johnstown Flood"

RUINS FROM SITE OF THE HULBURT HOUSE.

A 19ᵗʰ century illustration of flood damage

George M. Graham, a doctor aboard the passenger train driven by John Hess, also witnessed the disastrous scene, though not from the safe location that Mueller enjoyed. He knew something was wrong when the train first reversed its course and Hess began sounding that whistle in its continuous cry of alarm. He reported, "I stepped on the platform of one of the gondola cars, and looking east of the river, I saw what appeared like a bank of water coming with fearful velocity. Rolling at great height in its passage it showed trees, roots and bodies of trees, with debris of all kinds. I ran about fifty yards up the street, took a long breath, and, upon turning around, saw a building half way across the street at the point I had passed not thirty seconds before. The next instant it dashed against the corner and was surrounded by five or six feet of water. The force of the water lifted up and dashed the buildings one against another. The roaring of the rushing, fearful water, the tumbling and crashing of the buildings, and the wailing and cries of the women and children, no pen can describe. One poor woman came to me in agonizing distress, with her gaze so intent as if to pierce the water, crying out, 'Oh my baby! My dear baby is in the water!'"

While it would be easy to wonder why people didn't just get out of the way of the water, it is important to remember that not only did they have little to no warning, but they also were completely shocked by what they were seeing. Mary Butler later wrote, "Somewhere about 4 o'clock my sister happened to go to the window, and she heard a man passing, saying that the reservoir was broken. Then she said that we must take mother upstairs. So, we at once carried her upstairs and put her on the bed, which was a roped bedstead. I had barely time to rush downstairs to save something off the bed, which I succeeded in getting, that I could rescue from the rising water. Having secured those things, sister came downstairs and hurried me, grabbing hold of my hands, when the rising waters pushed me up, and I had barely time to get on the bed, when, pushed by the waters, the bed arose, bearing us with it within some eighteen inches of the ceiling. We all stayed in that condition all night; and although our house had been moved about a square from its foundation, we did not discover that fact until sometime during the night. During the night the chimney, which had been for some time tottering and threatening to fall upon us, eventually took a sudden start and fell through the lower roof, crushing the bedstead on which my mother had lain; and thus we also escaped that danger."

As Butler mentioned, some of the houses lifted up and moved so gently in the water that those inside didn't even know what had happened. She wrote, "During the night some neighbors called to us and asked if we were all there; and then they asked us if we knew where we were; and not till that time did we know that our house had been moved from its foundations, and was now in the middle of the street."

Like Louise Mueller, Gertrude Quinn felt that the flood had the look of a Biblical revelation. The sights that she saw stirred up memories of scenes that she had previously only seen through the eyes of religious artists: "I can never forget what I saw! It was like the Day of Judgment I have since seen pictured in books. Pandemonium had broken loose, screams, cries, and people were running: their white faces like death masks; parents dragging children, whose heads bobbed up and down in water; a boat filled to capacity with eager anxious passengers; household pets of all descriptions dangling from loving arms,' a wagon loaded to the breaking point lost a wheel and the despairing mortals riding therein where dumped down in a heap in the filthy water. They scrambled to their feet in less time that it takes to tell it, as the onrushing mob moved rapidly forward bent on self-protection at any cost. Animals and humans with eyes bulging out of their heads struggled to keep their feet against the horde and the weight of the water. They were all compressed into a solid mass that fairly wedged its way up the street, all straining every nerve and muscle to reach the hill, as the grim reaper stalked in the rear, and in the distance the mist and unmistakable rumblings telling in a new language what had happened. Bells were ringing, the whistles in the mills were sounding a last warning and intermingled with these were the shrill sounds from steam engines as throttles were opened for the last time; and now a moving mass black with houses, trees, boulders, longs and rafters coming down like an avalanche."

As is so often the case during times of crisis, faith proved to be an important factor in the lives of many of those who survived that day. This was even truer during the 18th century than it is today. A Mrs. S.W. Fields wrote, "We had not been in the attic fifteen minutes when someone said: 'There is Mrs. Tittle on a roof.' Then began the work of breaking the windows. Some of the men got a plank across to Mr. Joseph's roof, their house having moved some twenty feet, but could not strike us, for the reason that we were on a terraced lot, four feet above the street. Who were the first brought in I cannot tell, but in a very short time the attic was full. Some cried, some prayed, and I waited, feeling that this was God's time now. We, I then thought, had had our time. Dick, Albert, and Anna were standing with me. Dick asked: 'Mother, will we die?' I answered: 'I cannot tell; but one thing I do know, that God does all things well, and if He wanted us tonight He will take us; if not, He will find a way for our escape. We will go and sit down, and see what the Lord will do,' which we did, and Dick never asked another question."

Chapter 7: Fathers, Mothers, Children, All

"Fathers, mothers, children, all,
Both the young, old, great and small,
Were thrown about like chaff before the wind
When that fearful raging flood,
Rushing where the city stood,
Leaving thousands dead and dying there behind." – Joseph Flynn, "The Johnstown Flood"

Picture of a houses almost totally destroyed by the flood

Alexander N. Hart was one survivor who later wrote of his family's rooftop voyage: "When the flood struck my house it began to tremble and move. I took my two little boys, ages respectively 2 and 8 years, by the hands and leaped with them from the second-story window upon a floating roof. My wife and sister followed us. After being whirled by the surging waters we were driven against Rev. Dr. Beale's house, where the family were huddled in his attic story. He helped us into the room, which our addition made more crowded. The fierceness of the flood and the sight of tumbling houses made us fear that our refuge would soon fall. We then determined, if possible, to escape over the floating and accumulating roofs and wreck to Alma Hall."

Alma Hall was the tallest building in Johnstown, and one of the best built. During the night of the flood, more than 260 people ended up there, huddled together against the onslaught. Hart went on to describe how he and those with him made their way there: "Dr. Beale procured a rope, with which he let us down upon the roof of a floating house, which we secured to his residence. There were about twelve persons, women and children, besides Dr. Beale, Mr. Lloyd, and myself. Dr. Beale was the last to leave the attic, having secured our escape. With great labor we made our way over the roofs and debris. Strewed upon and fastened in the wrecks were the dead and wounded and dying. It was a heartrending sight, and we did what we could on our way to help or comfort the sufferers. Among these I recognized Mrs. Young (since deceased), her daughter Rose and son-in-law, J. Fleming. We finally got into Alma Hall, where we spent the night amid scenes that are too sad to recall."

As is always the case in situations like the Johnstown flood, many of the most horrific stories involved families with children. Henry Viering described his struggle to save himself and those he loved: "I was at home with my wife and children when the alarm came. We hurried from the house, leaving everything behind us. As we reached the door, a friend of mine was running by. He grasped the two smallest children, one under each arm, and then hurried on ahead of us. I had my arm around my wife's waist supporting her. Behind us we could hear the flood rushing. In one hurried glance as I passed a corner I could see the fearful flood crunching and crackling the houses in its fearful grasp, with no possibility of escape, as we were too far away from the hillside. In a flash I saw my three dear children licked up by it and disappear from sight, as I and my wife were thrown in the air by the rushing ruins. We found ourselves in among a lot of drift, driving along with the speed of a racehorse. In a moment or two we were thrown with a crash against the side of a large frame building, whose walls gave away as if they were made of paper, and the timbers began to fall about us in all directions."

What followed was an incident so unspeakable in its tragedy that words can hardly do it justice: "Up to this time I retained a firm hold on my wife; but I found myself pinned between two heavy timbers, the agony causing my senses to leave me momentarily; I recovered instantly, in time to see my wife's head just disappearing under water. Like lightening I grasped her by the hair, and as best I could, pinioned as I was above the water by the timber, I raised her above it. The weight proved too much, and she sank again. Again I pulled her to the surface, and again she sank. This I did again and again without avail. She drowned in that grasp, and at last dropped from my nerveless hands, to leave my sight forever! As if I had not suffered enough, a few moments later I saw white objects whirling around in an eddy until, reaching again the current, they floated past me. My God! Would you believe me? It was my children, all dead! Their dear little faces are before me now – distorted in a look of agony – that, no matter what I do, haunts me. Oh, if I could only have released myself at that time, I would have willingly gone with them! I was rescued sometime after, and have been here ever since. I have since learned that my friend, who so bravely endeavored to save two of the children, was lost with them."

Mr. Morrell Swank told an equally tragic tale: "When the great flood struck my residence at No. 312 Main Street I was on the second floor with my wife and two children and servant girl. My house was crushed like an egg shell right over our heads. My little son Roy was crushed to death in my arms." He went on to write, "Just when I thought my last moment had come, the water raised the house and pushed us upward through the ceiling. In a few moments we were carried down a considerable distance below the Kernville Bridge. My wife and I were only about four feet from each other, and she had the baby in her arms. I succeeded in getting loose, and took the baby from my wife and put it on a house-roof that was floating alongside of us. I then reached over to help my wife on the roof. Just then the water commenced to back up from the stone bridge, and I was whirled around out of reach of my wife, who drifted away, and she was drowned right before my eyes. Imagine my feelings when floating on the water about fifty feet deep, and houses crushing all around me loaded with human freight, the city under water, the Catholic church burning, and the rain coming down in torrents. The baby and I were finally rescued about a quarter of a mile up the Stony Creek. My servant girl, wife, son, parents, one brother and a sister were drowned, and only three of their bodies have been recovered."

Picture of the debris on Main Street

The Bridge of Death, Johnstown, Pa. U. S. A.

Another picture of debris near the stone bridge

Chapter 8: Houses Piled on High

"Soon houses piled on high,
Reaching far up to the sky
And containing dead and living human freight
Loud shrieks and groans soon rent the air,
From the wounded laying there,
With no chance to help avert their dreadful fate" – Joseph Flynn, "The Johnstown Flood

Picture of the home of the Sisters of Charity of Seton Hill

Pictures of damaged houses

Fortunately, not every story from the flood is as tragic as Viering's and Morrell's. Mrs. Fields reported, "Then I heard the call to come to the attic, which we all did with one accord. We had just reached it when I heard a terrible scream and breaking of glass. It was Miss Ida Hamilton, who screamed. She came to the attic, fell on her knees and thanked God for her escape, and also that her mother had been saved (in the house at the other side of theirs). Mrs. Henry, from Market Street, and her family, made a very narrow escape. Just as their house, with the family on the roof, came past the market-house, it fell, throwing them so that they were not over it for weeks. Mrs. McClay had left one of her servants, Mary Manealy, behind, which they lamented very much. Mrs. Henry insisted that, as their house came past Mrs. McClay's, they saw someone in the attic, on her knees; and about 4 o'clock, or just as soon as they could see, Mr. Murphy went across the roofs and found old Mary Manealy, safe and sound, wrapped up in Lizzie Tittle's fur-lined circular."

The incident brought out the best in many people, inspiring them to help others around them, especially the children, many of whom were facing a very uncertain future, as least for a while. Fields continued, "The little boy of B.F. Hills fretted all night for his papa and sister (she being drowned). He found his father next day on the hill. Mrs. Tittle brought in with her two little children, who had been taken in the afternoon at her house for safety; so when the big wave came she kept them. Their parents found them next day."

Fortunately, most of those coping with the crisis were not children but adults, who at least had some idea as to what to do. For instance, W.B. Tice related the following anecdote: "I heard a roar like thunder, one crash after another in quick succession, and on looking out of the window I beheld the most horrible sight I ever saw, and I hope I never may be called upon to witness such a scene again. The room I was in quickly filled with water, and in an instant I climbed on the roof by the aid of the spouting. The wall of water which came rushing toward me carrying everything before it seemed to be thirty feet in height, and in an instant, crash! and our building was raised aloft and whirled away by mad, rushing, bounding and boiling waters of the Little Conemaugh. Eight men were on this roof, and all around us were screaming hundreds of men, women and children. Many of them were swept into eternity; some were praying, some weeping and wailing and some cursing."

Fortunately, in addition to saving his own life, Tice was able to help others around him survive. He explained, "I was determined to keep my presence of mind and save myself and all others that I could. We sailed about three squares when the building struck the large brick store of Wood, Morrell & Co. I clung to the roof until it passed the store, when I leaped into the water and swam to a lumber pile, which floated into slack water up the Stoney Creek, where I had a full view of the terrible disaster. The Wire Mills and Gautier Works fell, crushing all in their way. Whole families of my acquaintance were entirely wiped out of existence. All this time I was still floating around, and finally I was caught by the wild waters and whirled away and over the now famous stone bridge of the P. R. R. At this time the clock struck 4, and I then thought I would never hear the clock strike again.... I was again compelled to jump, and after being knocked about until almost exhausted, I reached another housetop, sailing at the rate of about fifteen miles an hour; but, getting close to shore, I again jumped, and a mill man caught hold of my hand and assisted me to land; he was terribly excited and could not speak. I helped him to take two more men out."

The construction of homes in the 19th century certainly impacted the number of lives lost. While modern man has something of a romantic idea of the solidly built homes of yesteryear, the truth is that many were built quickly and by people who had little idea about what they were doing. What is worse is that even those that were well built lacked any attachment to their foundations; they simply sat on top of them. Victor Heiser's stable was soon floating rather than standing on his property: "In the path of the revolving stable loomed suddenly the house of our neighbor, Mrs. Fenn. To avoid being hurled off by the inevitable collision, I leaped into the air at the precise moment of impact. But just as I miraculously landed on the roof of her house, its wall began to cave in. I plunged downward with the roof, but saved myself by clambering monkey-like up the slope, and before the house gave way completely, another boiled up beside me. I caught hold of the eaves and swung dangling there, while the weight of my body drained the strength from my hands. For years thereafter I was visited by recurring dreams in which I lived over and over again that fearful experience of hanging with my fingernails dug deep into the water softened shingles, knowing that in the end I must let go. When my grip finally relaxed, I dropped sickeningly into space. But once again I was saved. With a great thud I hit a piece of the old familiar barn roof, and I clutched with all my remaining power at the half inch tin ridges. Lying on my belly, I bumped along on the surface of the flood, which was crushing, crumbling, and splintering everything before it. The screams of the injured were hardly to be distinguished above the awful clamor; people were being killed all about me."

Experiencing a disaster has a strange way of making small details clear in one's mind. Heiser, then only 16 years old, would subsequently recall with surprising clarity the shocking sights that he witnessed that day. "In that moment of terrible danger I saw the Italian fruit dealer Mussante, with his wife and two children racing along on what seemed to be their old barn floor. A Saratoga trunk was open beside them, and the whole family was frantically packing a pile of possessions into it. Suddenly the whole mass of wreckage heaved up and crushed them out of existence." Still, as horrific as what he saw was, he was unable to divert his attention from his fight for survival: "I was borne headlong toward a jam where the wreckage was already piling up between a stone church and a three story brick building. Into this hurly burly I was catapulted. The pressure was terrific. A tree would shoot out of the water; a huge girder would come thundering down. As these trees and girders drove booming into the jam, I jumped them desperately, one after another. Then suddenly a freight car reared up over my head; I could not leap that. But just as it plunged toward me, the brick building gave way, and my raft shot out from beneath the freight car like a bullet from a gun. In a moment more I was in comparatively open water. Although no landmark was visible, I could identify the space as the park which had been there only a short while before. I was still being swept along, but the danger had lessened."

It was during this period that Heiser learned the meaning of the old adage that sometimes a person has to laugh to keep from crying: "I had opportunity to observe other human beings in equally perilous situations. I saw the stoutish Mrs. Fenn astride an unstable tar barrel which had covered her with its contents. Rolling far over to one side, then swaying back to the other, she was making a desperate but grotesque struggle to keep her head above the water. There was nothing I could do for anybody."

Chapter 9: A Fearful Cry Arose

"But a fearful cry arose,
Like the screams of battling foes
For that dreadful sick'ning pile was now on fire
While they poured out prayers to heav'n,
They were burned as in an oven,
And that burning heap had formed their funeral pyre." – Joseph Flynn, "The Johnstown Flood"

Heiser soon found himself among those saved by the famous Stone Bridge: "I was carried on toward the narrows below the city where the tracks of the Pennsylvania Railroad crossed both valley and river on a high embankment and bridge. When the twisted, interlaced timbers ahead of me struck the stone arches, they plugged them tight, and in the powerful recoil my raft was swept back behind the hill which had saved the lower part of the town from complete destruction and left many buildings standing. I passed close by a two and a half story brick dwelling which was still remaining on its foundations. Since my speed as I went up this second valley was about that of a subway train slowing for a stop, I was able to hop to the roof and join the small group of people already stranded there. Realizing then that I was, perhaps, not immediately destined for the other world, I pulled out my watch. It was not yet four-thirty; three thousand human beings had been wiped out in less than ten minutes."

Picture of damage in the lower part of Johnstown a few days after the flood

Picture of a schoolhouse where survivors found refuge

Unfortunately, the pile of debris at the bridge soon became the most dangerous spot in the dying town, as the pile of wet wreckage somehow caught fire. While this may seem nearly impossible, it is important to remember that many of the houses and other buildings swept along contained stores of kerosene and other highly flammable materials. These spilled over the boards and branches and soon ignited them. Suddenly, those who thought they might have escaped the worst part of the flood found themselves in a blazing inferno. W.B. Tice remembered, "I went up on the embankment and looked across the bridge, which was filled full of debris, and on it were thousands of men., women and children, who were screaming and yelling for help, as at this time the debris was on fire, and after each crash there was a moment of solemn silence, and then those voices would be again heard crying in vain for the help that came not. At each crash hundreds were forced under and slain. I saw hundreds of them as the flames approached throw up their hands and fall backward into the fire, and those who had escaped drowning were reserved for the more horrible fate of being burned to death. At last I could endure no more. I climbed the hillside where I could see the church on fire close to the house where I had left my wife, but I could not see the house, and did not know she was safe. A more terrible and lonesome night alone in the woods and rain I never spent, knowing that my friends mourned me as dead and I thought they were all lost."

In all, 80 people died on the island pyre the debris had created. Even then, however, the fire was not over. In fact, it continued to burn for three more days, casting an eerie light over the recovering. Even after the first was out, the burned timbers left behind were so bound up in barbed wire from the factory that they could not be removed. After three months of concerted effort to clear the area, the railroad finally sent in a team of men with dynamite to blow it up.

Tragically, there was one other group of people who thought they were safe only to die suddenly. The train on the Pennsylvania Railroad tracks that ran through the city was unable to stop in time to save its passengers. Tice continued, "I remember one incident while I was on the housetop: a train of cars consisting of three or four coaches came puffing along the curve, and dashing into the water gave two puffs and was swept under the mad, rushing torrent."

By the time the fire at the Stone Bridge had died down, people were beginning to emerge from the places where they had weathered the disaster to take stock of their surroundings. Mrs. Fields remembered, "When we came out the next morning, we walked on planks laid on the sideboard, the upholstered chairs and extension tables through Mrs. Harshberger's house, over the roofs of some of the houses that were broken up. As I went I looked across to the hill that we were going to for refuge, and same some men carrying someone on a stretcher. They were to where I was going, and upon inquiry I found she was the wife of Mahlon Speck, who had been confined Thursday night; and on Friday, when the big wave came, she had to be taken to the attic. She lay there all night without a light and no one with her but her husband. Saturday morning some men carried her out over the roofs of the houses; and when I left her, on Monday morning, she was doing well. In Mr. Canan's attic there were sixty-nine persons. Of this number there were eighteen or twenty children. One of the men went out and got a load of dry bread, which was divided among the little ones and it was from Friday morning until Saturday noon that no food crosses our lips."

Picture of damage near Rail Road St.

While some found comfort in small morsels of food, others gave themselves over to trying to process what had just happened. The Reverend H.L. Chapman, pastor of the Franklin Street Methodist Church, recorded what he saw when the waters receded: "I went to the window and looked out on a scene of utter desolation. The water, from eighteen to thirty feet deep, had spread like a lake all over the better part of town in the direction of the railroad bridge. Only one dwelling house, that of Dr. Lowman, on the corner of the park remained. On the left several large buildings, which stood on Main Street, had escaped being protected by our large stone church, which had not only resisted the force of the flood, but parted the waters so as to save the bank building, the Presbyterian and Christian Churches and Alma Hall… But in the direct course of the flood, the large market house, the Episcopal Church, the large brick residence of Dr. L. T. Beam, and hundreds of others, showed no signs of ever having existed. The very trees in the park had been swept away, and an indescribable scene of desolation spread in every direction. To add to the general horror, the Catholic Church, to the east of us, burned fiercely, and the mass of debris, accumulated at the railroad bridge, had caught fire, and cast a lurid light over the devastated city, otherwise shrouded in gloom…"

Picture of debris stacked 40 feet high on Main St.

Picture of the damaged St. John's Church

Chapter 10: The Cry of Distress

"Then the cry of distress,
Rings from East to the West,

And our whole dear country now is plunged in woe
For the thousands burned and drowned
In the city of Johnstown,
All were lost in the great overflow." – Joseph Flynn, "The Johnstown Flood"

A picture of the debris in the aftermath

A picture of debris near the Merchant's Hotel

The entire area would remain "shrouded in gloom" for months to come. In all, 99 families were lost in their entirety. Nearly 400 children were killed. Among those who survived their lost loved ones were more than 300 newly made widows and widowers and almost 100 orphans. In total, more than 2,000 people were killed, the largest loss of civilian life in American history up until that time.

After such a disaster, the survivors wondered what to do next. People for miles around had lost their homes and businesses. Those passengers who had survived the train wreck were not homeless but instead were stranded miles from their homes. One of those caught far from home was the Reverend L.H. Leeper, who noted, "The few houses and a United Brethren church remaining in Conemaugh were kindly thrown open to give shelter to the homeless not washed away and the passengers saved from the trains. (A Mr. Devlin's home was my lodging place.) About four o'clock next morning the church bell suddenly rang out on the stillness, creating consternation anew among those who had escaped the perils of the evening before. Some word had gone around that the lake was but partially emptied and a second edition of the flood might come thundering down the valley at any moment. It proved, however, a less calamity."

Leeper went on to describe the aftermath he witnessed: "Three-fourths of the town of Conemaugh is so completely erased that a stranger would think it to have once been the bed of a river, from which the river had receded having washed for itself another channel. A little below Conemaugh was the borough of Woodvale, a village of modest homes belonging to their occupants, who as employees in the iron and steel works had from their wages saved and built for themselves, their wives and families, these cozy little homes. These houses – the wives and mothers and the children- all disappeared as the dust before the broom in the hand of a heartless giant. The site of Woodvale is a sandy waste or the bottom of a river! And its inhabitants mostly over yonder, never to return in time!"

During his stay in the area, Leeper spent much of his time exploring the site of the disaster and recording his observations for posterity. He was one of the first outside witnesses to reveal what had taken place in Johnstown, writing with the startling clarity of a man looking at other people's homes, not his own: "When the flood reached Johnstown it was divided into three awful currents, each about one square wide. These three seething volumes of wrath went tearing, washing, thundering right down through the city, dealing out ruin and terror in their pathway to an extent and with a fury unknown in modern times. Frame buildings were lifted up as by the hands of giant furies and either dashed to pieces against one another or sent tumbling and swimming on the bosom of the foaming current. The strong stone bridge stood with unyielding fidelity against the inconceivable force of these currents. Here the floating mass of houses, trees, logs, cattle, sheep, horses and human bodies were piled up far into the air in one awful conglomerate mountain pyre. The stables to two horse-car companies containing ninety horses were in that pile. Young men from the country had driven in to see the swollen river and hitched their teams to the street racks. These are all in that pile and their drivers "are not." for the flood took them! This huge pile took fire and burned for several days till the fire engines from Pittsburgh, after a persistent effort, succeeded in extinguishing it. There were many living persons wedged in among the broken timbers of that pile, whose screams were only hushed by the cruel flames!"

One of the first jobs at hand was the gruesome task of identifying and burying the dead. This was made more difficult by the fact that so many families had been wiped out in their entirety so that there was no one left to recognize the faces of those gone. More than 775 people remained unidentified until, their bodies proving to be a health hazard, they were finally buried in Westmont's Grandview Cemetery in a mass grave known as the "Plot of the Unknown." Mary Butler's brother was likely one of the unfortunates laid to rest in that place, as she later wrote, "Brother John had been running all the morning between our house and his sister's, Mrs. Long, who resided on Vine Street in Johnstown. At dinner time brother John said to mother, 'You will have to get some warm clothes on and get ready to go upstairs, as the water is rising and may come into the first floor.' … My brother John who had gone to town was never again heard of by us, nor has his body been recognized amongst the many that have been discovered and buried."

Pictures of people sifting through the wreckage

In addition to the loss of human life, there was the matter of the property loss and damage. More than 1,600 homes were destroyed, making the Johnstown Flood the worst in American 19th century history. Numerous businesses were plowed under the deluge, including Cambria Iron and Steel. The latter, fortunately, was able to rebuild and was again running up to speed within 18 months. This proved critical because most of those who survived the flood chose to stay in the area. Perhaps it was not so surprising, for it was, after all, the place they called home.

Picture of relief efforts after the flood

Bibliography

Beale, Reverend David. *Through the Johnstown Flood*. Philadelphia: Hubbard Brothers, 1890.

Cambria County Transit Authority. *Floods: 1889, 1936, 1977*. Johnstown: Benshoff, 1988.

Degen, Paula and Carl. *The Johnstown Flood of 1889: The Tragedy of the Conemaugh*. Eastern Acorn Press, 1984.

Law, Anwei. *The Great Flood*. Johnstown: Johnstown Area Heritage Association and the National Park Service, 1997.

McCullough, David G. *The Johnstown Flood*. New York: Simon and Schuster, 1968.

McLaurin, J.J. *The Story of Johnstown*. Harrisburg: James M. Place, 1890.

Pennsylvania Railroad Company. *Testimony Taken by the Pennsylvania Railroad, 1889-1891*.

Pryor, Elizabeth. *Clara Barton: Professional Angel*. Philadelphia: University of Pennsylvania, 1987.

Shappee, Nathan D. *A History of Johnstown and the Great Flood of 1889: A Study of Disaster and Rehabilitation*. Doctoral dissertation, University of Pittsburgh, 1940.

Slattery, Gertrude Quinn. *Johnstown and Its Flood*. Wilkes-Barre, 1936.

Strayer, Harold. *A Photographic Story of the Johnstown Flood of 1889*. Johnstown: Benshoff, 1964, 1993.

Printed in Great Britain
by Amazon